A PEANUTS CHRISTMAS

BY CHARLES M. SCHULZ

BALLANTINE BOOKS • NEW YORK

A Ballantine Book
Published by The Ballantine Publishing Group
Copyright © 2002 by United Feature Syndicate, Inc.

www.ballantinebooks.com
www.snoopy.com

Library of Congress Control Number: 2002094135

ISBN 0-345-45351-4

Book Design by HRoberts Design
Jacket Design by United Media

Manufactured in the United States of America

First Edition: November 2002

10 9 8 7 6 5 4 3 2 1

4

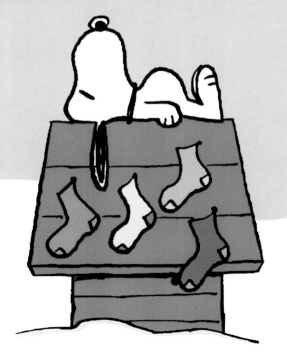

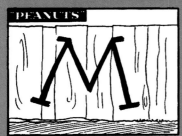

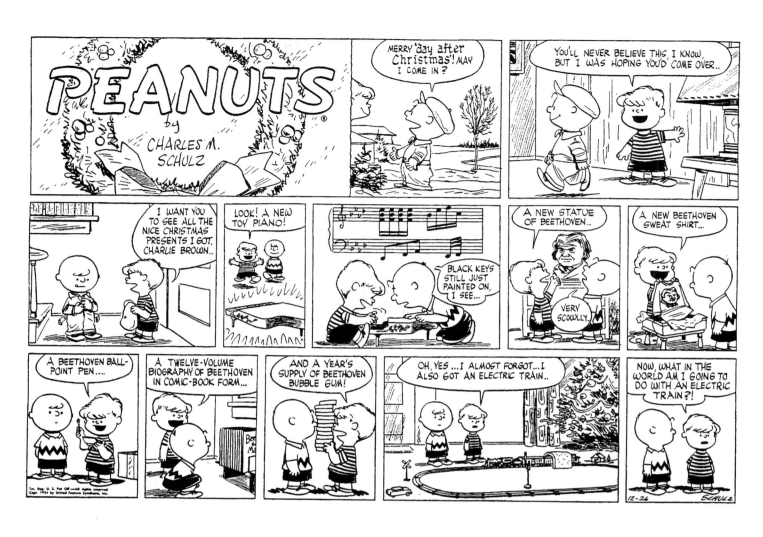

10

12-20

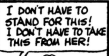

PEANUTS

YOU CAUGHT THE "MAD PUNTER"?

YUP, WE TRACKED HIM DOWN IN THE NEW-FALLEN SNOW...

WHAT DID YOU DO TO HIM?

NOTHING!

NOTHING?

IT'S ONLY RIGHT TO SHOW COMPASSION ON CHRISTMAS EVE!

12-24

PEANUTS

DEAR SANTA CLAUS, HOW HAVE YOU BEEN? HOW IS YOUR WIFE?

I AM NOT SURE WHAT I WANT FOR CHRISTMAS THIS YEAR.

SOMETIMES IT IS VERY HARD TO DECIDE.

11-16

PERHAPS YOU SHOULD SEND ME YOUR CATALOGUE.

SCHULZ

PEANUTS

DEAR SANTA CLAUS, ENCLOSED PLEASE FIND LIST OF THINGS I WANT FOR CHRISTMAS.

ALSO, PLEASE NOTE INDICATION OF SIZE, COLOR AND QUANTITY FOR EACH ITEM LISTED.

HOW EFFICIENT CAN YOU GET?

11-18   SCHULZ

PEANUTS

I'VE GOT THIS WHOLE SANTA CLAUS BIT LICKED, CHARLIE BROWN!

IF THERE **IS** A SANTA CLAUS, HE'S GOING TO BE TOO NICE NOT TO BRING ME ANYTHING FOR CHRISTMAS NO MATTER **HOW** I ACT...RIGHT? **RIGHT!**

AND IF THERE **ISN'T** ANY SANTA CLAUS, THEN I HAVEN'T REALLY LOST ANYTHING! RIGHT?

WRONG! BUT I DON'T KNOW WHERE!

12-13   SCHULZ

PEANUTS THIS IS MY "GIT" LIST, CHARLIE BROWN..

THESE ARE ALL THE THINGS I FIGURE I'M GONNA "GIT" FOR CHRISTMAS FROM MY TWO GRAMPAS AND TWO GRAMMAS AND EIGHT UNCLES AND AUNTS!

WHERE'S YOUR "GIVE" LIST? MY WHAT?

I KNEW IT!

PEANUTS AND THEN, ON CHRISTMAS EVE, SANTA CLAUS COMES DOWN THE CHIMNEY..

HE LEAVES THE TOYS ON THE HEARTH, GOES BACK UP THE CHIMNEY AND FLIES OFF THROUGH THE AIR IN HIS SLED!

SOMEHOW, I SENSE AN ELEMENT OF DOUBT..

17

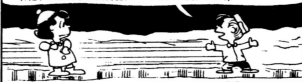

22

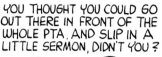

DEAR SANTA CLAUS, HOW HAVE YOU BEEN?

PLEASE DON'T GET THE IDEA THAT I AM WRITING BECAUSE I WANT SOMETHING.

NOTHING COULD BE FURTHER FROM THE TRUTH. I WANT NOTHING.

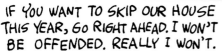

IF YOU WANT TO SKIP OUR HOUSE THIS YEAR, GO RIGHT AHEAD. I WON'T BE OFFENDED. REALLY I WON'T.

12-20

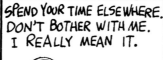

SPEND YOUR TIME ELSEWHERE. DON'T BOTHER WITH ME. I REALLY MEAN IT.

WHAT IN THE WORLD KIND OF LETTER IS THIS?!!

I'M HOPING THAT HE'LL FIND MY ATTITUDE PECULIARLY REFRESHING

SCHULZ

THAT ISN'T REALLY SANTA CLAUS..IT'S A DOG DRESSED UP LIKE SANTA CLAUS..

FOR THREE MONTHS I COUNTED THE DAYS UNTIL CHRISTMAS..

THEN LAST WEEK I STARTED TO COUNT THE HOURS...

THEN ON CHRISTMAS EVE I STARTED TO COUNT THE MINUTES; THEN THE SECONDS... I COUNTED EVERY SECOND UNTIL CHRISTMAS...

AND NOW IT'S ALL OVER!

GOOD GRIEF! I JUST REMEMBERED SOMETHING!

WE'RE SUPPOSED TO READ "GULLIVER'S TRAVELS" DURING CHRISTMAS VACATION, AND WRITE A REPORT ON IT! HAVE YOU STARTED YET?

STARTED? I DID MINE RIGHT AWAY SO I WOULDN'T HAVE TO WORRY ABOUT IT DURING VACATION

I HATE YOUR KIND!

CHRISTMAS VACATION IS ALMOST OVER..

I STILL HAVEN'T WRITTEN MY BOOK REPORT ON "GULLIVER'S TRAVELS."... I HAVEN'T EVEN STARTED TO **READ** IT YET!

WHY DON'T I GET STARTED? WHY DO I PUT THINGS OFF?

WHAT'S WRONG WITH ME?

30

PEANUTS featuring "Good ol' Charlie Brown" by Schulz

DECEMBER 25

DEAR GRAMPA AND GRANDMA,

WHAT ARE YOU DOING?

THANK YOU FOR THE CHRISTMAS PRESENT.

ARE YOU TRYING TO MAKE ME LOOK BAD?

I WAS REAL HAPPY TO GET THE DOLLAR.

YOU'RE WRITING A "THANK YOU" NOTE RIGHT AWAY JUST TO MAKE ME LOOK BAD, AREN'T YOU?

IT WAS VERY THOUGHTFUL OF YOU.

YOUR KIND DRIVE ME CRAZY! WHY DO YOU HAVE TO BE SO EFFICIENT?! WHY DO YOU HAVE TO...

LUCY ENJOYED HER GIFT, TOO, AND SAYS TO THANK YOU VERY VERY MUCH.

!

LOVE, Linus

IF YOU'LL WAIT A MINUTE, I'LL RUN AND GET YOU AN AIR MAIL STAMP!

12-25

33

35

38

"'Twas the month before Christmas"

39

I'M WRITING TO SANTA CLAUS..WHICH SHOULD I ASK FOR, A BICYCLE OR A DOG?

HERE IT IS!! I FOUND IT!

I FOUND THE WORD "SISTER" IN THE BIBLE!

THERE IT IS, RIGHT THERE! SEE? THERE'S THE WORD "SISTER" RIGHT THERE IN THE BIBLE!

SO?

THAT PROVES YOU HAVE TO GIVE ME A CHRISTMAS PRESENT!!!

OH, GOOD GRIEF!

I DON'T THINK I'LL TELL WOODSTOCK ABOUT SANTA CLAUS...

HE'LL NEVER GET ANY PRESENTS ANYWAY

SANTA CLAUS NEVER BRINGS PRESENTS TO TINY, NONDESCRIPT, NOBODY BIRDS

IT'S KIND OF SAD AT CHRISTMASTIME TO BE A NOBODY BIRD...

WHAT I REALLY SHOULD DO IS INVITE WOODSTOCK BACK TO THE DAISY HILL PUPPY FARM FOR CHRISTMAS

HE'D LIKE THAT...IT'S FUN TO GO HOME FOR CHRISTMAS...

BUT HOW CAN YOU GO HOME FOR CHRISTMAS WHEN YOUR HOME HAS BEEN REPLACED BY A SIX-STORY PARKING GARAGE?

GEE, THAT'S SAD!

PEANUTS
featuring
"Good ol' Charlie Brown"
by Schulz

POOCHIE?!

GUESS WHAT! YOU GOT A CHRISTMAS CARD FROM POOCHIE!

OH, NO!!

I'LL BET YOU DIDN'T SEND HER ONE, DID YOU?

OF COURSE, I DIDN'T... I WOULDN'T SEND POOCHIE A ROCK!

SHE WROTE A LITTLE NOTE ON THE BACK OF THE CARD...

I DON'T WANT TO HEAR IT!

"DEAR SNOOPY, I HOPE YOU HAVE A NICE CHRISTMAS...I THINK I AM GOING TO BE OUT YOUR WAY SOON...I'LL TRY TO STOP BY...SAY HELLO TO CHARLIE BROWN"

IF SHE COMES WITHIN A THOUSAND MILES OF ME, I'LL SCREAM!

IT'LL BE KIND OF NICE TO SEE POOCHIE AGAIN

SEEING POOCHIE AGAIN WOULD BE LIKE GETTING THE MUMPS TWICE!

YOU'VE NEVER FORGIVEN HER HAVE YOU?

12-24

YOU DON'T FORGIVE SOMEONE WHO DOES TO YOU WHAT SHE DID TO ME!

ANYWAY, HERE'S THE CARD..

I'LL BET SHE DOESN'T EVEN REMEMBER WHAT HAPPENED..

THAT WOULD BE JUST LIKE HER NOT TO REMEMBER...SHE'LL COME TO SEE ME, TOO... I KNOW SHE WILL...

JUST WHAT I DIDN'T NEED...A POOCHIE CHRISTMAS!

CLANG CLANG CLANG CLANG CLANG

PEANUTS I HATE TO SAY THIS, BUT YOU'VE BEEN VERY CRABBY SINCE CHRISTMAS

ANYONE WHO IS AT ALL SENSITIVE IS BOUND TO HAVE A POST-CHRISTMAS LETDOWN!

12-28

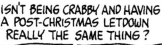

ISN'T BEING CRABBY AND HAVING A POST-CHRISTMAS LETDOWN REALLY THE SAME THING?

NOT AT ALL!!

PEANUTS Dear Santa Claus, Do not bring me any presents this year.

12-17

I want my Christmas to be one of peace and love, not greed.

Getting a lot of presents is for the birds

THAT'S ONLY AN EXPRESSION!!

PEANUTS DON'T GIVE ME ANYTHING FOR CHRISTMAS THIS YEAR, BIG BROTHER...

ALL I WANT IS FOR EVERYONE TO HAVE PEACE, JOY AND LOVE

12-18

DO YOU REALLY MEAN THAT? ARE YOU SINCERE?

NO, I THINK I'VE FINALLY FLIPPED!

PEANUTS IF YOU'RE TYPING YOUR CHRISTMAS LIST, YOU CAN SCRATCH ME... I DON'T WANT ANY PRESENTS THIS YEAR

12-19

Linus van Pelt
Sally Brown

Xxxxx xxxxxxxx

TAP TAP
TAP
TAP TAP
TAP TAP
TAP

SCRATCHING IS ONE THING... OBLITERATING IS ANOTHER!

PEANUTS I DON'T WANT YOU TO GIVE ME ANYTHING FOR CHRISTMAS THIS YEAR, LINUS...

REALLY? THAT'S TOO BAD, BUT I CAN UNDERSTAND HOW YOU FEEL, AND I ADMIRE YOU FOR IT...

12-20

CANCEL THAT ORDER FOR THE TEN-THOUSAND DOLLAR **NECKLACE**!!!

AFTER THE HOLIDAYS ARE OVER AND EVERYTHING HAS QUIETED DOWN, I'M GOING TO SLUG YOU!

46

50

PEANUTS featuring "Good ol' CharlieBrown" by SCHULZ

The Gift

It was the holiday season.

She and her husband had decided to attend a performance of King Lear.

It was their first night out together in months.

During the second act one of the performers became ill.

The manager of the theater walked onto the stage, and asked, "Is there a doctor in the house?"

Her husband stood up, and shouted, "I have an honorary degree from Anderson College!"

12-22

It was at that moment when she decided not to get him anything for Christmas.

SCHULZ

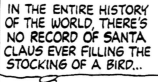

Dear Snooty Claus,

PEANUTS
featuring
"Good ol' Charlie Brown"
by Schulz

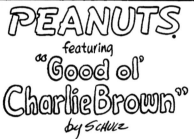

Dear Santa Claus,

ACTUALLY, THERE IS NO SANTA CLAUS...

This year please bring me a camera, a pony and a bicycle

THERE COMES A TIME WHEN WE HAVE TO STOP TRUSTING CERTAIN LEGENDS

some money, a desk, a goldfish, a record player, a bracelet,

AS WE GROW OLDER, WE HAVE TO FACE LIFE'S REALITIES

12-5

a hair dryer, a radio, a portable TV and some sweaters and jeans.

MYTHS HAVE TO BE REPLACED BY TRUTH

DO YOU WANT ME TO PUT YOU DOWN FOR A BASEBALL GLOVE?

YES, THAT WOULD BE VERY NICE

and a baseball glove for my brother.

'TIS THE SEASON TO BE WISHY-WASHY!

56

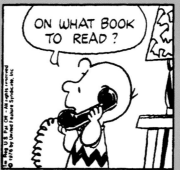

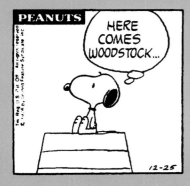

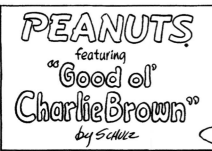

58

12-26

60

"THIS IS MY CHRISTMAS STORY..." SANTA AND HIS RAIN GEAR"

" WHEN SANTA LEFT THE NORTH POLE THAT EVENING, A GENTLE MIST WAS FALLING"

12-19

"IN HIS YELLOW SLICKER AND BIG RUBBER BOOTS, HE SET OUT ON HIS ANNUAL JOURNEY"

"IT WAS CHRISTMAS EVE, AND SOON CHILDREN AROUND THE WORLD WOULD BE HEARING THE SOUND OF SANTA AND HIS RAIN GEAR"

"LITTLE GEORGE WAS WAITING FOR SANTA TO COME"

" SUDDENLY HE HEARD THE SOUND OF SOMEONE WALKING ON THE ROOF! IT WAS A MAN IN A YELLOW SLICKER AND BIG RUBBER BOOTS!"

12-20

"'I SAW HIM!' SHOUTED LITTLE GEORGE.. 'I SAW SANTA AND HIS RAIN GEAR'"

DON'T SQUIRM, MA'AM, THERE'S MORE TO COME!

" THE RAIN CAME DOWN HARDER AND HARDER"

"BUT THE MAN IN THE YELLOW SLICKER AND BIG RUBBER BOOTS NEVER FALTERED"

12-21

"ANOTHER CHRISTMAS EVE HAD PASSED, AND SANTA AND HIS RAIN GEAR HAD DONE THEIR JOB! THE END"

HA HA HA! HA HA! HA HA!

THEY SURE HAD THEIR NERVE LAUGHING AT MY STORY..... HA!

HOW ABOUT THIS THING WITH ALL THE REINDEER PULLING THE SLEIGH THROUGH THE AIR? NO WAY!

12-23

I DON'T CARE HOW MANY REINDEER HE HAD, THEY COULD NEVER PRODUCE ENOUGH LIFT TO GET A SLED IN THE AIR...

NO WAY, HUH, BIG BROTHER? NO WAY! MERRY CHRISTMAS!

THERE'S THE HOUSE WHERE THAT LITTLE RED-HAIRED GIRL LIVES...

MAYBE SHE'LL SEE ME, AND COME RUSHING OUT TO THANK ME FOR THE CHRISTMAS CARD I SENT HER...MAYBE SHE'LL EVEN GIVE ME A HUG...

MAYBE BILLIE JEAN KING WILL CALL ME TONIGHT, AND INVITE ME OUT TO DINNER

Dear Santa Claus, How have you been?

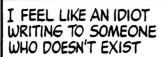
I FEEL LIKE AN IDIOT WRITING TO SOMEONE WHO DOESN'T EXIST

ON THE OTHER HAND, IF HE REALLY DOES EXIST AND I DON'T WRITE, I'D FEEL EVEN DUMBER!

THIS IS THE TIME OF YEAR WHEN IT'S BEST TO TOUCH ALL BASES

WHATEVER THAT MEANS

CHRISTMAS WILL BE HERE BEFORE WE KNOW IT

I'VE MADE UP A LIST OF THINGS YOU MIGHT WANT TO GIVE ME...

DIDN'T MISS A BEAT

CHRISTMAS IS COMING, CHARLIE BROWN

I'VE MADE OUT A LIST TO HELP YOU DECIDE WHAT TO GET ME

WELL, MY HANDS ARE FULL RIGHT NOW..COULD YOU PUT IT SOME PLACE WHERE I'LL REMEMBER IT?

I'VE MADE UP A NEW LIST OF THINGS I WANT FOR CHRISTMAS, CHARLIE BROWN

I HATE TO ADMIT IT, BUT I CAN'T EVEN REMEMBER WHERE WE PUT THE OTHER LIST

DON'T WORRY, I KNOW JUST WHERE IT IS...

JOE SPINDLE!

HOW WOULD YOU LIKE TO SEE A LIST OF THINGS I WANT FOR CHRISTMAS?

ABSOLUTELY NOT! I WANT MY GIFT TO YOU THIS YEAR TO BE A COMPLETE AND DELIGHTFUL SURPRISE

WHAT A LOVELY GENEROUS THOUGHT... ＊SNIF＊

OFF THE OL' HOOKEROO!

Panel 1: DID I SEE YOUR FAMILY TAKING DOWN YOUR CHRISTMAS TREE YESTERDAY?

Panel 2: ALL THE DECORATIONS AND ORNAMENTS HAVE BEEN PACKED AWAY, AND EVERYTHING CLEANED UP

Panel 3: HOW ABOUT YOU?

Panel 4: I HAVEN'T SENT OUT MY CARDS YET!

Panel 5: ADDRESSING YOUR CHRISTMAS CARDS, HUH, BIG BROTHER?

Panel 6: THAT'S A GOOD IDEA

Panel 7: Merry

Panel 8: DO YOUR CHRISTMAS SMUDGING EARLY!

I want my Christmas to be one of peace and love, not greed.

WHY DOES SHE TAKE ME ON' THE BACK OF HER BICYCLE WHEN SHE GOES SHOPPING?

IT'S NOT AS IF THIS IS A STATION WAGON OR A PICKUP...

12-10

THERE'S NO ROOM TO CARRY ANYTHING...

EXCEPT A FEW CHRISTMAS TREE ORNAMENTS...

I HAVE A SUGGESTION, MA'AM...YOU KNOW WHAT WOULD MAKE A PERFECT GIFT TO YOUR CLASS?

DON'T ASSIGN US A BOOK TO READ DURING CHRISTMAS VACATION!

WHAT DO YOU SAY, MA'AM?

EVEN MY SUGGESTIONS GET A "D MINUS"!

12-12

© 1990 United Feature Syndicate, Inc.

Dear Joe Claus,

12-13

"SANTA"   WHAT?

HIS NAME IS "SANTA," NOT "JOE"

I DIDN'T THINK THAT LOOKED RIGHT

I AGREE...ONE OF THE GREAT JOYS IN LIFE IS GOING INTO THE WOODS, AND CUTTING DOWN YOUR OWN CHRISTMAS TREE...

12-17

THAT'S TRUE...THERE'S NO SENSE IN CUTTING DOWN THE FIRST ONE YOU SEE...

© 1990 United Feature Syndicate, Inc.

SNOOPY AND HIS LITTLE FRIEND WENT INTO THE WOODS TO CUT DOWN A CHRISTMAS TREE

THAT STUPID BEAGLE! DOESN'T HE KNOW YOU CAN'T JUST GO INTO THE WOODS, AND START CUTTING DOWN TREES?!

12-18

WHY NOT? WHO'S GOING TO CARE?

I NEVER REALIZED THAT SQUIRRELS COULD GET SO UPSET...

MA'AM, ABOUT THIS BOOK YOU WANT US TO READ DURING CHRISTMAS VACATION..

12-19

IS IT AN INTERESTING BOOK?

I SEE

I HATE IT WHEN SHE SAYS, "THAT'S FOR ME TO KNOW, AND YOU TO FIND OUT"

"AND LAID HIM IN A MANGER BECAUSE THERE WAS NO ROOM FOR THEM IN THE INN.".. LUKE 2:7

SOME SCHOLARS FEEL THAT THE "INN" MORE LIKELY WAS A PRIVATE HOME WITH A GUEST ROOM

12-20

"MANGER" COULD ALSO BE CONFUSING HERE SO SOME SCHOLARS THINK THAT PERHAPS THE...

WOULDN'T IT BE NEAT TO HAVE A CHRISTMAS TREE COMPLETELY COVERED WITH JUST CANDY CANES?

ONCE THEY GET SCRATCHED OFF MY CHRISTMAS LIST, THEY NEVER GET BACK!

HAVE YOU EVER BEEN SCRATCHED OFF A CHRISTMAS LIST?

I'M NOT SURE

IF YOU EVER ARE, THAT'S WHAT IT WILL LOOK LIKE!

I DON'T KNOW WHAT TO GET YOU FOR CHRISTMAS

YOU'RE A HARD ONE TO SHOP FOR..

NOT REALLY

I CAN ALWAYS USE MORE TRACK FOR MY ELECTRIC TRAIN...

THIS IS THE HOLIDAY SEASON

IF YOU WERE SMART, YOU'D WRITE A NICE CHRISTMAS STORY...

11-26

It was a dark and stormy Christmas night.

YOU SHOULD WRITE A SENTIMENTAL CHRISTMAS STORY..

IT SHOULD BE SAD, BUT VERY INSPIRING...

11-27

IT ALSO SHOULD HAVE A CHARACTER IN IT THAT EVERYONE WILL LOVE

"Tiny Jim"

HOW MANY MORE SHOPPING DAYS UNTIL CHRISTMAS?

TWENTY!

WHAT DID YOU TELL ME THAT FOR?

BECAUSE YOU JUST ASKED ME!

12-1

I REALLY DIDN'T WANT TO KNOW

Dear Santa Claus,

OKAY, NOW YOU TELL ME WHAT YOU WANT HIM TO BRING YOU, AND I'LL PUT IT IN THE LETTER...

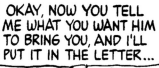

WHAT COLOR?

I'M PRACTICING DRAWING CHRISTMAS WREATHS

THEY LOOK MORE LIKE DOUGHNUTS TO ME

DUNK A CHRISTMAS WREATH IN A CUP OF COFFEE, AND YOU'RE IN TROUBLE!

I'M GOING TO TRY TO SELL CHRISTMAS WREATHS FROM DOOR TO DOOR

GETTING ON THE OL' COMMERCIAL BANDWAGON, EH? GOING AFTER THOSE BIG HOLIDAY BUCKS, HUH?

NEED ANY HELP?

GUESS WHAT.. I'VE BEEN ASKED TO BE IN THE CHRISTMAS PLAY!

I'M GOING TO BE AN ANGEL

ALL I HAVE TO DO IS SAY, "HARK!"

I'M GLAD THEY DIDN'T ASK ME.. I WOULD HAVE SAID, "BARK!"

THIS IS WHAT I HAVE TO DO IN THE CHRISTMAS PLAY

WHEN THE SHEEP ARE THROUGH DANCING, I COME OUT AND SAY, "HARK!"

12-16

THEN HAROLD ANGEL STARTS TO SING

© 1983 United Feature Syndicate, Inc.

HAROLD ANGEL?

IT'S RIGHT HERE IN THE SCRIPT...

"HARK!" HOW DID THAT SOUND? I'M PRACTICING MY LINE FOR THE CHRISTMAS PLAY

I LIVE IN MORTAL DREAD OF GETTING OUT ON THE STAGE AND FORGETTING WHAT I'M TO SAY...

12-17

WELL, IF YOU DID, YOU COULD ALWAYS MAKE UP SOMETHING

© 1983 United Feature Syndicate, Inc.

THAT'S TRUE.. HOW ABOUT, "HEY!"

NOT VERY BIBLICAL..

HERE'S THE LINE I HAVE TO SAY IN THE CHRISTMAS PLAY... SEE IF I CAN GET IT RIGHT...

© 1983 United Feature Syndicate, Inc.

HARK!

YOU GOT IT

12-19

I'VE ALWAYS WONDERED HOW ACTORS REMEMBER ALL THOSE LINES...

I'M ALL SET FOR THE CHRISTMAS PLAY..DO I LOOK LIKE AN ANGEL?

YOU LOOK FINE... ARE YOU GOING TO WALK TO THE AUDITORIUM LIKE THAT?

CAN YOU GET YOUR COAT ON OVER YOUR WINGS?

© 1983 United Feature Syndicate, Inc.

NO PROBLEM

12-20

So far this has been a good Christmas play, Charlie Brown...

When does your sister come on?

Right after the dancing sheep...she steps out and says, "Hark!" and then Harold Angel sings

Harold Angel?

All I know is what she told me...

The sheep are through dancing, Charlie Brown.. here comes your sister...

Hockey stick!

"Hockey stick"?!?

I said, "Hockey stick!" Why did I say, "Hockey stick"? All I had to say was, "Hark!" and I said, "Hockey stick!"

I ruined the whole Christmas play! Everybody hates me! Moses hates me, Luke hates me...

..The apostles hate me..

All fifty of them!!

Look, Gramma sent us a Christmas card with a dollar in it..

"Twas the month before Christmas"

I DON'T KNOW...I DIDN'T SEE THE REST OF THE PLAY..AS SOON AS SALLY SAID, "HOCKEY STICK," AND EVERYONE LAUGHED, I LEFT

SHE GETS EVERYTHING MIXED UP...SHE EVEN THOUGHT SOMEONE NAMED "HAROLD ANGEL" WAS GOING TO SING!

EXCUSE ME, SOMEBODY'S AT THE DOOR...

HI, IS SALLY HOME? MY NAME IS HAROLD ANGEL..

WHEN IT COMES TO RIDING ON THE BACK OF MOM'S BICYCLE, I'M A WHITE KNUCKLE FLIER...

LOOK OUT FOR THE TREE! LOOK OUT FOR THE FENCE!

"JINGLE BELLS (LOOK OUT!) JINGLE (LOOK OUT!) BELLS (LOOK OUT!) JINGLE ALL THE (LOOK OUT!) WAY..."

SINGING DOESN'T HELP......

Dear Santa Claus,

DOES SANTA CLAUS HAVE A TITLE OR A RANK?

I DON'T KNOW..I'VE NEVER THOUGHT ABOUT IT..

I'LL PUT DOWN LIEUTENANT COLONEL

SO LONG, MILDRED! GOODBYE, DANNY! TOO BAD, ESTHER!

THESE ARE PEOPLE I'M SCRATCHING OFF MY CHRISTMAS CARD LIST

GET LOST, MABEL! THAT'S THE WAY IT GOES, FRED! BYE-BYE, JOE! FORGET YOU, LYDIA!

I'VE NEVER HAD SO MUCH FUN IN ALL MY LIFE!

I'M REALLY TRIMMING DOWN MY CHRISTMAS CARD LIST THIS YEAR...

MILDRED, DANNY, ESTHER, MABEL, FRED, JOE, LYDIA, VERNA, EMIL, FLOYD... I CROSSED 'EM ALL OFF!

I'M DOWN TO ONE LAST NAME...

© 1984 United Feature Syndicate, Inc.

AND THERE GOES JESSIE!!

"HARK!" HOW DID THAT SOUND? I'M PRACTICING MY LINE FOR THE CHRISTMAS PLAY

I LIVE IN MORTAL DREAD OF GETTING OUT ON THE STAGE AND FORGETTING WHAT I'M TO SAY...

12-17

WELL, IF YOU DID, YOU COULD ALWAYS MAKE UP SOMETHING

© 1983 United Feature Syndicate, Inc.

THAT'S TRUE.. HOW ABOUT, "HEY!"

NOT VERY BIBLICAL..

YES, MA'AM, I'D LIKE TO VOLUNTEER TO PLAY THE PART OF MARY IN OUR CHRISTMAS PLAY...

YOU WHAT?

12-18

THAT'S RIGHT, SIR.. SHE ASKED ME YESTERDAY

© 1984 United Feature Syndicate, Inc.

MARY NEVER WORE GLASSES!!

HEY, CHUCK.. DID MARY EVER WEAR GLASSES? WHAT DO YOU MEAN, "MARY WHO?"

12-19

IN THE BIBLE! DOES IT SAY ANYTHING ABOUT MARY WEARING GLASSES?

THEN HOW CAN MARCIE PLAY MARY INSTEAD OF ME, AND THE TEACHER SAYS I'M GOING TO BE PLAYING A SHEEP?!!

© 1984 United Feature Syndicate, Inc.

WHY CAN'T I EVER BE A WRONG NUMBER?

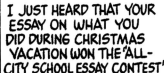

GOOD MORNING! THIS IS A CHRISTMAS WREATH, AND...

11-22

THANK YOU! I LOVE SAMPLES!

SLAM!

I GIVE UP! I CAN'T IMAGINE ANYONE ELSE HAVING AS MUCH TROUBLE AS I DO SELLING CHRISTMAS WREATHS...

Dear Santa Claus, I saw a recent picture of you in a magazine.

12-3

You look fatter than ever.

I know how you usually fly through the air with your reindeer and sleigh.

I'll be surprised this year if you even get off the ground.

YOU KNOW WHY I DON'T WANT YOU TO BUY ME ANYTHING FOR CHRISTMAS THIS YEAR?

BECAUSE I KNOW YOU HATE ME!

I'VE NEVER SAID I HATE YOU...

12-5

THEN BUY ME SOMETHING!!

88

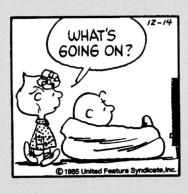

YES, MA'AM, HE WANTS TO RETURN THIS BOOK HE GOT FOR CHRISTMAS

HE DOESN'T LIKE IT BECAUSE THE HERO IS A CAT...

HE HATES CATS

BLEAH!

12-26

HE WANTS A BOOK WHERE ALL THE CATS GET EATEN BY ALLIGATORS ON THE FIRST PAGE!

Dear Snoopy,
Did you have a nice Christmas?

12-27 © 1985 United Feature Syndicate, Inc.

I bought myself something I have always wanted.

Even though I have to admit that where I live it isn't very practical.

Dear Grandma,
Thank you for all the nice Christmas presents.

Everyone in our family liked their gifts.

© 1985 United Feature Syndicate, Inc.

Even my dog.

12-28

He says to thank you for the Beagleneck sweater.

DID BEETHOVEN EVER BUY HIS GIRLFRIEND FUZZY MITTENS FOR CHRISTMAS?

I DOUBT IT..

HERE'S YOUR CHANCE TO DO SOMETHING HE NEVER DID...

I'VE ALREADY THOUGHT OF DOING SOMETHING HE NEVER DID...

12-2

KLUNK!

Dear Santa Claus, I hope this letter reaches you before Christmas.

12-13 © 1986 United Feature Syndicate, Inc.

I am worried about something.

When you come to fill my stocking...

Please be careful. Love, Spike

MA'AM?

I WAS WONDERING IF YOU'D LET US MAKE SOME PAPER CHAINS FOR OUR CHRISTMAS TREE..

YOU KNOW, AS SORT OF A CLASS PROJECT..

12-16

WE COULD START WITH MY MATH PAPER..

Dear Santa Claus,

Dear Mr. Claus,

Dear Monsieur Claus,

Dear Santa Claus,

12-13

BECAUSE I SAID SO, THAT'S WHY!

Dear Grandma,
How have you been?
By the way, thanks for
the Christmas present.

PEANUTS by Schulz

"FOUR CALLING BIRDS, AND A PARTRIDGE IN A PEAR TREE.." | THAT SONG DRIVES ME CRAZY!

WHAT IN THE WORLD IS A "CALLING BIRD"? | A CALLING BIRD IS A KIND OF PARTRIDGE..

IN I SAMUEL, 26:20, IT SAYS, "FOR THE KING OF ISRAEL HAS COME OUT TO SEEK MY LIFE JUST AS THOUGH HE WERE HUNTING THE CALLING BIRD..."

THERE'S A PLAY ON WORDS HERE, YOU SEE.. DAVID WAS STANDING ON A MOUNTAIN CALLING, AND HE COMPARED HIMSELF TO A PARTRIDGE BEING HUNTED...

ISN'T THAT FASCINATING?

12-20

IF I GET SOCKS AGAIN FOR CHRISTMAS THIS YEAR, I'LL GO EVEN MORE CRAZY!

SEE? I'M MAILING ALL MY CHRISTMAS CARDS..

IS THE ONE YOU'RE SENDING TO ME IN THERE, TOO?

RIGHT THERE IN THE OL' MAILBOX..

SCHULZ 12-19

WOW!

© 1987 United Feature Syndicate, Inc.

HERE.. ONE OF YOUR CHRISTMAS CARDS CAME BACK.. IT SAYS, "NO SUCH ADDRESS"

IT'S THAT GIRL AT SCHOOL! SHE'S GOING TO DRIVE ME CRAZY!!

12-21

WHY DO YOU BOTHER WITH HER?

SCHULZ © 1987 United Feature Syndicate, Inc.

SHE FASCINATES ME!

MAY I ASK YOU A SIMPLE QUESTION?

TODAY MY NAME IS SARAH..

OKAY, SARAH.. PLEASE TELL ME HOW I CAN SEND YOU A CHRISTMAS CARD IF YOU GIVE ME THE WRONG ADDRESS...

12-22

LAST YEAR WE HAD ALL BLUE LIGHTS ON OUR TREE..

SCHULZ © 1987 United Feature Syndicate, Inc.

I THINK THIS ONE IS FOR YOU..

OH, NO! IT'S A CHRISTMAS CARD FROM LYDIA!

12-23 © 1987 United Feature Syndicate, Inc.

YOU DIDN'T SEND HER ONE, DID YOU?

I COULDN'T! SHE WOULDN'T EVER TELL ME HER ADDRESS!

I'VE BEEN OUT-CHRISTMASED!!

SCHULZ

DON'T TALK TO ME..
I'M HAVING MY
POST-CHRISTMAS LETDOWN

I JUST WANTED TO
THANK YOU AGAIN FOR
THE WONDERFUL PRESENT
YOU GAVE ME...IT WAS
JUST WHAT I WANTED...

RATS!

WHY DO YOU ALWAYS
HAVE TO SAY
SOMETHING NICE?

HI, LYDIA.. I THOUGHT ABOUT YOU A LOT DURING CHRISTMAS VACATION

THANK YOU FOR THE NICE CHRISTMAS CARD.. I REALLY WANTED TO SEND YOU ONE, TOO, YOU KNOW..

1-4-88

I STILL CAN'T FIGURE OUT WHY YOU WOULDN'T GIVE ME YOUR ADDRESS

TODAY MY NAME IS MELISSA!

THIS YEAR I'M GOING TO MAKE ALL MY CHRISTMAS PRESENTS.. AND GUESS WHAT I'M GIVING EVERYBODY..

PAPER AIRPLANES!

11-25

YOU'RE LUCKY.. YOU GOT YOURS EARLY!

I VOLUNTEERED TO WRITE OUR CLASS PLAY FOR CHRISTMAS..

IN THE OPENING SCENE GERONIMO TALKS TO MARY..

IT WASN'T GERONIMO.. IT WAS GABRIEL...

11-29

REALLY? THE KID WHO PLAYS GERONIMO IS GOING TO BE VERY DISAPPOINTED..

I HEAR YOUR CHRISTMAS PLAY WAS CANCELED

THE SCHOOL BOARD DID US IN..

I THOUGHT I WROTE A GOOD PLAY, TOO..

12-6

MY BEST SCENE WAS WHERE JOSEPH DRIVES HIS FAMILY TO EGYPT IN A '56 THUNDERBIRD..

LOOK, KID, DON'T BLAME ME... BLAME THE SCHOOL BOARD! NO, WE'RE NOT GOING TO HAVE A CHRISTMAS PLAY...

12-7

NO, YOU'RE NOT GOING TO BE GABRIEL OR GERONIMO OR ANYBODY! YOU HAD ALL YOUR LINES MEMORIZED?

WELL, FORGET 'EM.. RUB AN ERASER ON YOUR HEAD!

I'M SORRY YOUR CHRISTMAS PLAY WAS CANCELED..

NO CHRISTMAS PLAY..NO CHRISTMAS TREE..NO CHRISTMAS CAROLS..NO CHRISTMAS COOKIES...

12-8

JUST A MATH TEST ON RED AND GREEN PAPER..

HEY, KID, GUESS WHAT.. THERE'S GONNA BE A COMPROMISE...

THEY SAY WE CAN HAVE A CHRISTMAS PLAY AS LONG AS THERE'S NO RELIGION IN IT..

12-9

HOW WOULD YOU LIKE TO BE GERONIMO?

I'M WONDERING IF YOU'D LIKE TO ADDRESS ALL MY CHRISTMAS CARDS FOR ME

DID I SEND A CHRISTMAS CARD TO MARLA LAST YEAR?

YES, I REMEMBER BECAUSE YOU SAID SHE DIDN'T SEND YOU ONE

I THINK I'LL SEND HER ONE ANYWAY...

12-19

MAYBE IT'LL MAKE HER FEEL BAD..

12-20

How I Spent My Christmas Vacation

Worrying about this stupid assignment.

12-21

PEANUTS by SCHULZ

IT'S NOT GOING TO HAPPEN..

?

NOT FOR US!

THERE'S NO USE GETTING YOUR HOPES UP..

WE'RE THE LOWEST OF THE LOW..

OLD SANTA CLAUS COULDN'T CARE LESS ABOUT CREATURES LIKE US!

WE DON'T COUNT FOR ANYTHING! THAT OLD GUY DOESN'T KNOW WE EVEN EXIST...

?

© 1989 United Feature Syndicate, Inc.

WOW! I CAN'T BELIEVE IT!

THERE'S A CARD, TOO? WHAT DOES IT SAY?

"MERRY CHRISTMAS FROM THE NEW IMPROVED SANTA CLAUS"

12-24

I KEEP TRACK OF ALL THE PEOPLE WHO DIDN'T SEND ME A CHRISTMAS CARD, AND THEN I HOLD A GRUDGE AGAINST THEM

YOU LOOK PUZZLED...

WAIT 'TIL I SHOW YOU MY LIST OF PEOPLE WHO DIDN'T GIVE ME ANY PRESENTS..

I DON'T THINK YOU'RE THE REAL SANTA CLAUS..

IF YOU'RE THE REAL SANTA, WHERE ARE YOUR HELPERS?

THAT'S THE DUMBEST THING I'VE EVER SEEN!

WHO CARES? MERRY CHRISTMAS, SWEETIE! WOOF, WOOF, WOOF!

FOR ME? THANK YOU VERY MUCH

"FOR THE ROUND-HEADED KID.. MERRY CHRISTMAS"

IT WOULD BE NICE TO HAVE A DOG WHO REMEMBERED YOUR NAME

YOU KNOW WHY I WANT TO BUY PEGGY JEAN THOSE GLOVES FOR CHRISTMAS?

WHEN I FIRST MET HER THIS SUMMER AT CAMP, I NOTICED WHAT PRETTY HANDS SHE HAD... I WANT THOSE PRETTY HANDS TO BE WARM..

12-4

BUT I DON'T HAVE TWENTY-FIVE DOLLARS TO BUY THE GLOVES...

SEND HER A NICE CARD, AND TELL HER TO KEEP HER HANDS IN HER POCKETS!

SEE? THERE THEY ARE... THOSE ARE THE GLOVES I'D LIKE TO BUY PEGGY JEAN FOR CHRISTMAS..

WHERE ARE YOU GOING TO GET TWENTY-FIVE DOLLARS?

THAT'S THE PROBLEM

MAYBE YOU COULD SELL YOUR DOG...

12-5

I TAKE IT BACK.. HE'S PROBABLY ONLY WORTH FIFTY CENTS

LUCY SAID IF I NEED TWENTY-FIVE DOLLARS TO BUY PEGGY JEAN A CHRISTMAS PRESENT, I SHOULD SELL MY DOG...

WHAT A GREAT IDEA!

THAT'S THE FIRST TIME I'VE EVER SEEN HIM SPILL HIS WATER DISH..

12/6

I FEEL GUILTY FOR NOT GIVING HIM ANYTHING..

DON'T WORRY ABOUT IT..HE CAN'T REMEMBER EVERYONE WHO WALKS BY..

DARK HAIR..BEADY EYES..CHECKERED COAT...

12-18

WHAT ARE YOU DOING?

I'M LEAVING A PLATE OF COOKIES UNDER OUR TREE FOR SANTA CLAUS

© 1990 United Feature Syndicate, Inc.

AND IF I HIDE SOMEPLACE, MAYBE I'LL EVEN GET TO SEE HIM...

IT WORKED! I SAW HIM!! I SAW SANTA CLAUS!

12-23

BUT I NEVER REALIZED HE WAS SO SHORT..

SCHULZ

ALL RIGHT, WHO CAN TELL ME SOMETHING ABOUT CHRISTMAS?

THE GREAT GATSBY USED TO THROW BIG CHRISTMAS PARTIES AT HIS HOUSE..

HE DID NOT! WHERE DO YOU GET THESE IDEAS?!

12-18

WHEN HE WAS LITTLE, GATSBY GOT A SLED FOR CHRISTMAS, AND HE CALLED IT "ROSEBUD"!

I CAN'T STAND IT!

ALL RIGHT, WHO CAN TELL ME WHY WE PUT A STAR ON TOP OF OUR CHRISTMAS TREES?

GATSBY USED TO LOOK ACROSS THE STREET AT THE GREEN STAR ON TOP OF DAISY'S TREE...

HE DID NOT! YOU STUPID KID!

12-19

YOU SHOULDN'T YELL AT SOMEONE JUST BEFORE CHRISTMAS

RERUN, AS YOUR BIG SISTER, I FEEL IT IS MY DUTY TO TELL YOU THAT WHAT YOU SEE IS NOT THE REAL SANTA CLAUS

WHAT YOU'RE LOOKING AT IS A DOG IN A SANTA CLAUS SUIT..

NOW THAT I'VE TOLD YOU THIS, HOW DOES IT MAKE YOU FEEL?

12-20

I LIKE HIM!

WOOF!

WHAT DID HE SAY?

12-21

"THANK YOU.. THE MONEY IS FOR A WORTHY CAUSE.. MERRY CHRISTMAS.. SAY 'HELLO' TO THE STUPID KID WITH THE BLANKET AND HIS CRABBY SISTER"

CLANG CLANG CLANG CLANG CLANG

HAVE YOU THOUGHT ABOUT WHAT YOU'RE GOING TO GET ME FOR CHRISTMAS?

CHRISTMAS WAS YESTERDAY

IT'LL BE HERE AGAIN BEFORE YOU KNOW IT..

12-26

Dear Grandma, Thank you for the

WHAT DID GRANDMA GIVE ME FOR CHRISTMAS?

WHICH GRANDMA?

ANY GRANDMA!

12/27

WHAT ARE YOU GOING TO BUY WITH THE MONEY YOU GOT FROM GRANDPA FOR CHRISTMAS?

I THOUGHT MAYBE I'D USE IT TO BUY A BOOK..

12-28

A **WHAT**?!

"D-MINUS"?! I GOT A "D-MINUS" FOR THE WHOLE YEAR?!!

YES, MA'AM, I'M VERY HURT... I THINK I DESERVED A BETTER GRADE..

6-1

OH, BY THE WAY...WHILE WE'RE TALKING...

HERE'S THE BOOK REPORT THAT WAS DUE LAST CHRISTMAS..

12-9

LOOK WHAT MOM PUT IN MY LUNCH FOR US... CHRISTMAS COOKIES!

WOW! A WHOLE BUNCH! TOO BAD WE DON'T HAVE SOMEONE TO SHARE THEM...

12-10

HERE, I THOUGHT YOU MIGHT LIKE A LITTLE SNACK WHILE YOU'RE WORKING..

12-11

HEY, LOOK, MA! SANTA CLAUS IS EATING OUT OF A DOG DISH!

PEANUTS by SCHULZ

WHERE'S A GOOD PEN?

I NEED SOME EXTRA NICE STATIONERY..

Dear Samantha Claus, How have you been?

SAMANTHA CLAUS?

SHE'S THE FAT LADY WITH THE REINDEER WHO BRINGS US CHRISTMAS PRESENTS

WITH THE RED SUIT AND THE WHITE BEARD?

THE WHITE BEARD IS JUST SORT OF A DISGUISE..

VERY CLEVER

12-13

© 1992 United Feature Syndicate, Inc.

HOW WOULD IT BE IF I ASKED HER TO BRING YOU A NEW BICYCLE?

WHY NOT?

Please bring my brother a new bicycle.

DOES SAMANTHA CLAUS GO, "HO HO HO!" OR DOES SHE JUST SMILE DAINTILY?

Forget the bicycle!!

SCHULZ

12-17

HERE'S AN INTERESTING ITEM FROM NEEDLES, CALIFORNIA...

SOMEONE SNEAKED INTO THE CHAMBER OF COMMERCE BUILDING LAST NIGHT, AND PLUGGED IN AN EXTENSION CORD

THE CORD LED OUT OF TOWN SOMEWHERE INTO THE DESERT..

EVERYONE IS PUZZLED AS TO WHO OR WHY SOMEONE SHOULD DO SUCH A THING..

12-18

!

12-19

NEEDLES CHAMBER OF COMMERCE

ALL RIGHT, WHO UNPLUGGED MY TREE ?!

HEY, MARCIE.. Y'GOT ANY EXTRA CHRISTMAS CARDS? I FORGOT TO BUY SOME..

AND HOW ABOUT STAMPS? I'LL NEED SOME STAMPS, TOO

12-22

HERE, KEEP THIS ONE.. THEN I WON'T HAVE TO SEND IT TO YOU...

© 1992 United Feature Syndicate, Inc.

IT'S GOOD TO SEE YOU FILLED WITH THE HOLIDAY SPIRIT, SIR..

'TIS THE SEASON TO BE SARCASTIC

12-23

I JUST REMEMBERED.. AREN'T WE SUPPOSED TO LEAVE SOMETHING UNDER THE CHRISTMAS TREE FOR SANTA CLAUS?

HOW ABOUT THIS FROZEN BROCCOLI?

© 1992 United Feature Syndicate, Inc.

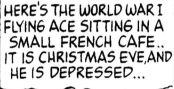

HERE'S THE WORLD WAR I FLYING ACE SITTING IN A SMALL FRENCH CAFE.. IT IS CHRISTMAS EVE, AND HE IS DEPRESSED...

12-24

..BUT I SHOULDN'T COMPLAIN.. WHAT ABOUT MY BROTHER SPIKE WHO'S OUT THERE IN THE TRENCHES?

© 1992 United Feature Syndicate, Inc.

I WONDER IF SPIKE IS THINKING ABOUT CHRISTMAS..

12-25 © 1992 United Feature Syndicate, Inc.

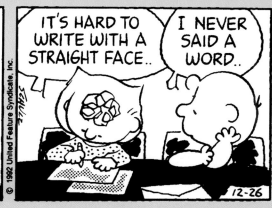

PEANUTS. *by Schulz*

WHERE ARE YOU GOING?

SANTA CLAUS IS DOWN AT THE CORNER..I HAVE A FEW QUESTIONS TO ASK HIM..

SO, MR. FANCY CLAUS, REMEMBER ME? MY NAME IS RERUN...

WHAT HAPPENED TO ALL THE THINGS YOU WERE GOING TO BRING ME FOR CHRISTMAS LAST YEAR? KIND OF FORGOT, DIDN'T YOU? HUH?!

I DON'T SUPPOSE YOU'D CARE TO EXPLAIN, WOULD YOU, HUH?!

© 1994 United Feature Syndicate, Inc.

ROWRR!!

12-4

HOW DID IT GO?

WE REALLY DIDN'T TALK THAT MUCH..HE SEEMED PRETTY BUSY..

I THOUGHT IT MIGHT BE NICE TO DROP A LITTLE NOTE TO SANTA CLAUS'S WIFE..

Dear Signora Claus,

"SIGNORA"?

I HAVE A THEORY THAT HE MARRIED A NICE ITALIAN GIRL..

RATS! NO ONE SENT ME A CHRISTMAS CARD..

WELL, DID YOU SEND ANY YOURSELF?

DID I WHAT?

DID YOU SEND ANY YOURSELF?

DID I WHAT?

SOMEDAY, I'M GOING TO LIVE IN A BIG HOUSE WITH A FIREPLACE, AND ON CHRISTMAS EVE I'LL HANG MY STOCKING ON THE FIREPLACE, AND SANTA CLAUS WILL COME AND FILL MY STOCKING WITH WONDERFUL PRESENTS...

IN THE MEANTIME, MY ARM IS FALLING OFF!

© 1994 United Feature Syndicate, Inc.

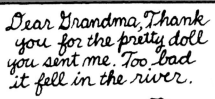

THERE! I'VE MAILED ALL MY CHRISTMAS CARDS!

I THOUGHT YOU DIDN'T HAVE ANY STAMPS..

I DREW MY OWN.. I DREW DICK TRACY, AND POPEYE, AND THE YELLOW KID..

THAT'S ILLEGAL

SOMEONE NEED AN ATTORNEY?

ALL MY CHRISTMAS CARDS CAME BACK!

THAT'S BECAUSE YOU DREW YOUR OWN STAMPS

I COPIED THEM FROM THE NEW CARTOON STAMPS

SHE DREW A BETTER POPEYE THAN THEY DID..

DO YOU THINK I'LL GET ARRESTED FOR DRAWING MY OWN STAMPS?

WELL, YOU MIGHT START LOOKING FOR A GOOD ATTORNEY..

BEFORE WE BEGIN, YOUR HONOR, MAY WE ASK IF YOU RECEIVED THE CHRISTMAS CARD WE SENT YOU?

YES, MA'AM.. I SORT OF NEED YOUR ADVICE..

DO YOU THINK I SHOULD SPEND THE ONLY DOLLAR I HAVE ON A CHRISTMAS PRESENT FOR A GIRL WHO DOESN'T KNOW I EVEN EXIST?

THANK YOU..

I JUST SAVED A DOLLAR..

WHY DON'T YOU GET RID OF THAT BELL SO YOU CAN HEAR WHAT I WANT FOR CHRISTMAS?

BONK!

THIS IS THE TIME OF YEAR WHEN I MISS THE DAISY HILL PUPPY FARM..

WE ALWAYS HAD A CHRISTMAS TREE..

IT'S HARD TO DECORATE A ROCK..

141

IF YOU'RE A REAL SANTA CLAUS, WHERE ARE YOUR REINDEER?

HOW ARE YOU GONNA LAND ON ALL OF THOSE ROOFTOPS AND GO DOWN ALL THOSE CHIMNEYS?

AND AFTER YOU GO DOWN A CHIMNEY, HOW ARE YOU GONNA GET BACK UP?

12-17

AND EVEN IF YOU DO, WHAT MAKES YOU THINK YOUR REINDEER WILL BE WAITING FOR YOU?

I'LL GIVE YOU ABOUT THREE HOUSES, AND YOU'LL BE COMPLETELY EXHAUSTED..

I THOUGHT YOU WERE PROBABLY DOWN HERE, BUT THEN I DIDN'T HEAR YOUR BELL ANYMORE..

CHRISTMAS IS COMING..YOU SHOULD ASK FOR A SLED..

I THOUGHT MAYBE I'D GET A DOG FOR CHRISTMAS, BUT I DIDN'T..

OWNING A DOG IS A BIG RESPONSIBILITY, RERUN..THEY NEED LOTS OF CARE..

AND THEY NEED A LOT OF COMFORTING..

1-2-96

I'M SENDING A CHRISTMAS CARD TO MICKEY MOUSE BECAUSE HE GAVE ME HIS SHOES..

Dear Mickey, Merry Christmas.

Thanks again for the shoes. Your friend, Spike

P.S. Just out of curiosity, why do you wear gloves all the time?

12-23

12-24

ASK YOUR MOM IF SHE'D LIKE TO BUY SOME HOMEMADE CHRISTMAS CARDS..

PEANUTS

by Schulz

"FOUR CALLING BIRDS, AND A PARTRIDGE IN A PEAR TREE.."

THAT SONG DRIVES ME CRAZY!

WHAT IN THE WORLD IS A "CALLING BIRD"?

A CALLING BIRD IS A KIND OF PARTRIDGE..

IN I SAMUEL, 26:20, IT SAYS, "FOR THE KING OF ISRAEL HAS COME OUT TO SEEK MY LIFE JUST AS THOUGH HE WERE HUNTING THE CALLING BIRD..."

THERE'S A PLAY ON WORDS HERE, YOU SEE.. DAVID WAS STANDING ON A MOUNTAIN CALLING, AND HE COMPARED HIMSELF TO A PARTRIDGE BEING HUNTED...

ISN'T THAT FASCINATING?

IF I GET SOCKS AGAIN FOR CHRISTMAS THIS YEAR, I'LL GO EVEN MORE CRAZY!

© 1987 United Feature Syndicate, Inc.

12-21-97

HELP HELP HELP

Dear Brother Snoopy, This year I had a great idea.

For my Christmas tree, I decorated a tumbleweed.

It looked really beautiful.

12-1-97

But then it left!

HE HAS THESE REINDEER, SEE, AND THEY FLY THROUGH THE AIR PULLING HIS SLED...

12-24-97

AND IF YOU BELIEVE THAT, I HAVE A GOLD BIRD NEST THAT I'LL SELL YOU FOR A DOLLAR!

HA HA HA HA!

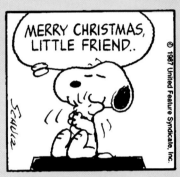
MERRY CHRISTMAS, LITTLE FRIEND..

© 1987 United Feature Syndicate, Inc.

I DECIDED TO WRITE A LETTER..

GOOD FOR YOU..

HOW DO YOU SPELL "BY THE WAY"?

JUST THE WAY IT SOUNDS.. "BY THE WAY"

8-10

www.snoopy.com

© 1998 United Feature Syndicate, Inc.

Dear Grandma, How have you been? By the way, thanks for the Christmas present.

PEANUTS by Schulz

SIGH

HELP ME, LINUS.. I WANT TO MAKE A SPECIAL CHRISTMAS CARD FOR THE LITTLE RED-HAIRED GIRL..

DRAW A TREE, CHARLIE BROWN, WITH SOME TINY RED HEARTS HANGING ON IT..

THEN WRITE SOMETHING SORT OF PERSONAL AT THE BOTTOM...

WHAT'S GOING ON? IS MY SWEET BABBOO HELPING MY BIG BROTHER DRAW A CHRISTMAS CARD?

I'M NOT YOUR SWEET BABBOO!!

© 1998 United Feature Syndicate, Inc.
12-20

THAT IS SO STUPID! THAT IS SO HUMONGOUSLY STUPID!

THERE! HOW DOES THAT LOOK? I DREW A TREE WITH LITTLE HEARTS ON IT..

"MERRY CHRISTMAS FROM YOUR SWEET BABBOO"?!

IT'S A FAMILY EXPRESSION..

YES, SIR..MY NAME IS RERUN..DID YOU KNOW THAT SANTA CLAUS IS GOING TO BRING ME A DOG?

SO WHAT I NEED IS A LEASH, AND A COLLAR, AND A SUPPER DISH...

12-21

AND YOU CAN JUST PUT IT ON MY TAB..

© 1998 United Feature Syndicate, Inc.

SNOOPY, WHO AM I KIDDING?

12-24

LUCY IS RIGHT..SANTA CLAUS IS NEVER GOING TO BRING A DOG TO SOMEONE WHOSE MOM DOESN'T WANT HIM TO HAVE A DOG..

IF I'M LUCKY, I'LL GET A PAIR OF SOCKS AND AN ORANGE..

IF I GET A RUBBER BONE, I'LL SHARE IT..

12-25

12-26

YOU HAVE TO UNDERSTAND.. I'M NOT COMPLAINING..

I UNDERSTAND..

© 1998 United Feature Syndicate, Inc.

I SIMPLY LEARNED THAT WE SHOULDN'T ALWAYS EXPECT TO GET EVERYTHING WE ASK FOR..

THAT'S CALLED "PREACHING TO THE CONVERTED"

Row 1:

Dear Grandma, Thank you for the money you sent me for Christmas.

I plan to save it for my college education

YOU SPENT IT ALL YESTERDAY..

Everyone says the sweater looks good on me.

12-28

Row 2:

REMEMBER, IF WE MEET SOMEONE ON THE SIDEWALK, SAY, "HAPPY NEW YEAR"

1-1-99

IF I SAY,"HAPPY NEW YEAR," WILL THEY GIVE ME A BICYCLE?

NO, THEY WON'T GIVE YOU ANYTHING

LET'S GO HOME..

Row 3:

Dear Snooty Claus,

"SNOOTY" CLAUS?

HE THINKS HE'S SO SMART.. HE DIDN'T BRING ME ANYTHING I WANTED LAST YEAR..

WELL, DON'T BURN YOUR BRIDGES..

BRIDGES? WHAT HAVE BRIDGES GOT TO DO WITH IT?

NOW I FORGOT WHAT I WAS WRITING..

11/30

MERRY CHRISTMAS, LITTLE FRIEND..

DO NOT OPEN UNTIL SOMEDAY

YES, MA'AM..I'D LIKE TO RETURN SOMETHING I BOUGHT HERE..

IT'S A CHRISTMAS PRESENT FOR A GIRL, BUT HE WAS TOO SHY TO GIVE IT TO HER..

IT WAS NEVER OPENED..

YES, I WAS GOING TO GIVE IT TO A LITTLE RED-HAIRED GIRL IN OUR CLASS..

YOU KNOW HER?

YOU'RE HER MOM?

YOU WORK HERE? IN THIS STORE? YOU'RE HER MOM, AND YOU WORK HERE?

WHEN WE FIRST SAW YOU, WE THOUGHT YOU WERE HER OLDER SISTER..

WHY DID YOU TELL HER THAT?

SHE LET YOU RETURN THE PRESENT, DIDN'T SHE?

156